A New Home

by Holly Harper

illustrated by Eva Katinka Bognar

OXFORD
UNIVERSITY PRESS
AUSTRALIA & NEW ZEALAND

Joe's mum and dad had rented a new home.

Joe loaded his computer games in a box.
It was time to go.

Joe gave a sad sigh.

Just then Mr Whiskers came in.

"What if my new room is not as big?"
Joe said to Mr Whiskers. "What if there
is no garden?"

"What if there are no children to play with?" Joe said. He felt sick inside.

Joe went to see Mum and Dad.

They had just finished packing.

The boxes went on a trolley. Mum and Dad
lifted the boxes into a van.

Joe got Mr Whiskers into his cat box.

"Let's go!" said Mum.

"I hope I like our new home, Mr Whiskers," said Joe in a whisper.

They arrived at the new home. The address was 1 August Drive.

Dad got out the key. They made their way inside.

"Our new home!" said Dad.

Mr Whiskers flew from his cat box.

"Take a look around, Joe," said Mum. "I will make us a snack."

Joe found his new room. He gave a smile.

The garden was big!

Mr Whiskers gave a mew. He had found a cute cat to play with.

Just then …

"You have found Newt!" said a girl. She was near the back gate. "I am Steph," she said.

Later that day ...

"Do you like our new home?" asked Mum.

"I do!" Joe said. "Mr Whiskers likes it too!"